To Jeremiah,

# Raise
# Your GPA

Be Encouraged.

*Jonathan*

# Raise Your GPA

## GOD'S WAY TO WIN @ SCHOOL & LIFE

**Jonathan Banks**

ISBN: 1544983565
ISBN-13: 9781544983561
Library of Congress Control Number: 2017905099
CreateSpace Independent Publishing Platform
North Charleston, South Carolina

# Dedication

*To every young person who cares about his or her future and to the hardworking parents who give their best to their sons and daughters every day.*

# Contents

# Preface

This book will help you win more at school and life. One of the ways it helps is by using God's Word, the Bible, to increase your wisdom and your faith. There are different translations of the Bible used throughout the book to help you get the most out of each chapter. If you want to know which translation is used, simply check each quote for the three-letter indicator. For example, NLT stands for the New Living Translation. A complete list can be found at the end of the book.

I have also included some Flash Cards, GPA Notes, and a special prayer at the end of the major chapters to help you remember some of the key points. Additional cards and other tools are posted on RaiseYourGPA.org.

Please consider sharing your experiences with this book with your friends, family, and online communities to help inspire as many people as possible. Use the hashtag #RaiseYourGPA and our handle @RaiseYourGPA whenever possible.

Enjoy.

# Acknowledgments

I thank God for everyone who believed in the experiences and gifts in my life and encouraged me to write this book.

To my wife and love of my life, Jacinta—Thank you for loving me and allowing me to love you. God spoils me through you and I will love you forever.

To Jonathan and Justin, our sons—Being your father is one of my greatest joys. I am amazed at the young men you are becoming as you love God, live courageously, and serve others.

To Bishop Horace Smith, MD and my AFC family— Your leadership and love have shaped me and my family. Our best days are ahead of us.

To my parents and family, who gave me their best and loved me for me—I know that God's love and plans for you are amazing.

To every young person, wherever you are—struggling or successful, your destiny motivates me to pray with you and inspires me to *Raise My GPA*. Thank you.

We will rise together.

# CHAPTER 1

# Guaranteed Success

What if you found a way to guarantee success in your life? How much would it be worth to you? How hard would you work for it?

First, let's figure out if you have the ingredients for success. **Spoiler alert**: being talented, gifted, smart, cute, and hardworking does not guarantee success.

We are not trying to find out if you have the **potential** to be successful—God gives opportunity to all of us. We are trying to discover how motivated you are to understand success and if you are willing to do what it takes to achieve it.

Are you ready to go beyond ordinary living and rise to true success?

True success is more than getting a college degree, a nice job, the right relationship or becoming famous. Although many of those things come with success, they don't define it. I have taken time with thousands of young people, and the best definition of success I can give you is this: **Success** is maximizing your **potential** and accomplishing your **assignments**.

It may seem a little weird talking about potential and assignments. After all, who gives and measures your potential? Who gives you your assignments? Ultimately God does - God, our loving Creator, Heavenly Father, and ultimate grader (judge). True success is the result of great preparation with a commitment to God and His plan for your life.

Because our lives start in God, we know that when we put godly thinking and godly priorities together with godly living, the result will always be true success. God designs us for success and gives us every opportunity to achieve it.

What we must understand is that God wants us to be successful and will help us every step of the way. Check out what God's Word says in Philippians 2:13: "For God is working in you, giving you the desire and the power to do what pleases him" (NLT).

This book is designed to help you reach your highest level of success in school and life. It's designed to raise your GPA.

You will find out more about your GPA in the upcoming chapters, but for now, think of your GPA as a way to measure your success. So let's get ready to rise!

## Success in God's Design

You are designed for success, not failure. That's why success and winning feel great, and defeat and failure feel horrible. When God told a young man named Jeremiah, "Before I formed you in the womb, I knew you. Before you were born, I set you apart for my holy purpose" (Jer. 1:5a, GWT), He was letting Jeremiah know that his life had meaning and significance. Jeremiah was not a mistake or unwanted, even though there were times when he felt alone and scared.

God told Jeremiah that He designed everything about him. God designed his nationality, his parents, his abilities, his appearance, his strengths, and his weaknesses. Jeremiah's design was intentional, and God designed him to accomplish a specific purpose and assignment.

Even though your design and purpose are different from Jeremiah's, you are just as important to God and His plan. Romans 2:11 says, "God does not show favoritism" (NIV). That confirms that God designs each of us for success—**no exceptions**! It feels good to know that God loves us and designed us to be winners.

## Success in God's Direction

God's Word gives us so much information about living great lives and being successful. However, there are many times when we don't know what to do or which path to take to find success. The Bible's book of wisdom, Proverbs, helps us out. Proverbs 3:5–6 says, "Trust in the LORD with all your heart; do not depend on your own understanding. Seek his will in all you do, and he will show you which path to take" (NLT).

When we search for God's direction, our search must begin with trusting God. Trust is relying on something or someone. There should be **nothing** and **no one** whom we trust more than God. But trusting God takes practice.

God never wants us to sin (disobey or offend God), hurt ourselves or others, or abandon our faith. Even when times are hard, God always wants us to reject sinful and selfish choices and trust Him by searching for His direction. Trusting God means choosing His way when it is not easy or convenient and when it doesn't make sense to our minds.

Trust is not blind. It's strategically placed in God, who has proven Himself as Creator, friend, Savior, and Almighty Lord.

When we "seek his will in all we do," meaning we purposely try to make God happy by our decisions and actions, God promises to guide our decisions and direct our lives. God's promises show us that we don't have to figure out and understand every part of God's plan to find success. When we have a decision to make or our life needs direction, we need to trust Him and His Word and look for the godly way to succeed.

"Commit your actions to the LORD, and your plans **will succeed**" (Prov. 16:3, NLT). That's not just success—it's God-guaranteed success!

## Success in God's Destiny

People love to quote Jeremiah 29:11: "'For I know the plans I have for you,' declares the LORD, 'plans to prosper you and not to harm you, plans to give you hope and a future'" (NIV). What most people miss about Jeremiah 29:11 is that God was letting His people know that He was directing the tough times they were experiencing. God was using the tough times to show them that He was in control and not them.

We must understand that we are responsible for our lives—how we use our time, talents, and resources. But we do not have ownership of our lives. Everything we are and have belongs to God. We are blessed to belong to God. When our relationship with God is healthy, meaning we love and serve Him with our whole hearts, the destiny that He designs will happen—100 percent guaranteed!

## Fun Fact

God's destiny is a **who**, not a **where** or a **what**. If God's destiny for you were a *where*, anyone could get there and probably before you. If it were a *what*, someone else could steal it or copy it. But God's destiny is a *who*, and that *who* is you. Not the *who* who stares at you in the mirror or the *who* who's been posting your selfies online; God's destiny for you is the person He's transforming you into. It's your God-designed character, integrity, strength, and faith. God's destiny for you is the person you're becoming.

God will use every experience, every victory, and every disappointment to shape your spirit and heart into the *you* whom He desires, the *you* the world needs, the *you* who loves like He loves, and the *you* who will ultimately make you so happy and fulfilled.

It's true. Check out Romans 8:28: "And we know that in all things God works for the good of those who love him, who have been called according to his purpose" (NIV).

With God's design, destiny, and direction, let's maximize everything God has given you. Do your best in every situation, and make the most of every opportunity. You will accomplish your assignments as you trust God and live with godly courage and passion.

Check out what God told another young leader named Joshua (Josh. 1:7–9, NLT):

Be strong and very courageous. Be careful to obey all the instructions Moses [Joshua's leader] gave you. Do not deviate from them, turning either to the right or to the left. Then you will be successful in everything you do. Study this Book of Instruction continually. Meditate on it day and night so you will be sure to obey everything written in it. Only then will you **prosper** and **succeed** in all you do. This is my command— be **strong** and **courageous**! Do not be afraid or discouraged. For the LORD your God is with you wherever you go.

God told Joshua how to maximize his potential and accomplish his assignments. Joshua needed to use what his mentor had taught him about God and His Word. We succeed when we read God's Word, think about it, prioritize it, and do it.

God promised that Joshua would be successful in "everything you do" when he "obey[ed] everything written in it." God is not saying that if you mess up or miss something, you'll be a failure. But when you use your strength and courage to trust God in everything, He guarantees success.

Since failure is not an option, go! Become everything God has designed you to be, and you'll do everything He has destined you to do. Guaranteed.

## GPA Thought

As you read this book, the choices you make in the next few moments and days can have an impact on how much success you experience throughout your life.

## Chapter 1 Prayer for Success

Lord God, I thank you for your amazing design, direction, and destiny in my life. I choose to trust you and your love so that I can accomplish every assignment that you have for me and maximize my godly potential. I choose your courage and strength over fear and failure. I love you for loving me and ask for your blessing in Jesus' name. Amen.

---

**Chapter 1 Flash Card**

## Success

Success is **maximizing** your potential and
**accomplishing** your assignments.

---

**Chapter 1 Flash Card**

## God's Design

God designs each of us for **success** in
His holy purpose.

---

**Chapter 1 Flash Card**

## God's Direction

Trust God through His Word and look for the godly way
toward **success**. God promises to direct your life.

---

**Chapter 1 Flash Card**

## God's Destiny

God's destiny for you is the person He's transforming you into
(the person you're becoming).

## GPA Notes

What does this chapter make you think about?

_____

_____

_____

_____

_____

_____

_____

_____

_____

In what areas of your life are you looking for greater success?

_____

_____

_____

_____

_____

_____

_____

_____

_____

_____

In what areas of your life do you need more of God's direction?

_____

_____

_____

_____

_____

_____

_____

_____

_____

How can you help others experience more success?

_____

_____

_____

_____

_____

_____

_____

_____

_____

# CHAPTER 2

## Raise Your GPA

On the road to success, there are twists, turns, confusing signs, dead ends, speed bumps, and all sorts of obstacles. Sometimes it can be hard to tell if you are winning or losing, growing toward success, or falling away from it.

In school, they measure your success by giving each grade a point value and dividing the number of points received by the total number of credit hours. This is called your grade-point average or GPA. Your school takes your grades from math, English, science, humanities, and other classes to calculate your GPA.

The higher your grade-point average, the better your academic standing. It affects which colleges and universities you will be accepted into, how much scholarship money you are eligible for, and how happy or sad you and your parents are at report card time.

With God, success is measured differently. God's Word tells us in Deuteronomy 6:5 that godly success comes through loving God with all your heart, soul, mind, and strength.

Matthew 22:37–40 and Mark 12:29–31 let us know that godly success also depends on how well you love others. Loving God and loving others are the two main parts of a godly life. These two make up another, more important GPA–your **God-point average**.

Your success in these two areas means everything to God. Measuring them shows you if you are winning or losing in life and ultimately affects your eternal reward.

Your God-point average measures whether you are moving closer to God or away from Him. It helps you stay focused on the most important opportunities you will ever have: to be born again and to live a life that pleases God.

So how do we get an A in loving God? First, let's clear up the difference between believing in God's existence and loving Him. Believing that there is a God is a good first step in having a successful relationship with Him and achieving success in life. But mere belief or acknowledging His existence doesn't impress anyone. God's Word says that there are evil spirits that believe in God and fear Him enough that they shake in awe of Him (James 2:19–20). That's not the type of faith that loves God.

If I say that I believe that I have a mother, but I never spend time with her or show love and kindness to her, and my feelings for her never affect her or anyone around me, what good is my belief? Does my saying I believe that I have a mother show her any kind of love? My mom wouldn't want that type of empty love, and neither would yours.

Bottom line: God will always love you with His A game—make sure you love Him with yours.

So how should we love God? We should love God by giving Him priority, preeminence, and preference in our lives.

## Love God by Giving Him Priority

One of the ways that you love God is by giving Him **priority** in your life. That means that God comes first in everything—your time, your reading, your money, your relationships, your music, your body...first in everything!

So many of us have our priorities lined up in our minds, but we fail to give our top priorities the time and attention they deserve. We can't say that God is number one in our lives but then allow everything else to come before Him.

Every one of us has 168 hours in every week. Some of us will choose to put God first in that time—setting aside time to pray, read God's Word, connect with other believers, and do everything else that leads to godly success.

Unfortunately, far too many of us fail to take time to pray, don't ever read our Bibles, and never connect with other believers in spiritually uplifting ways. Years ago, my fantastic wife taught me that people do what they want to do. They take time for their true priorities and show it with their time. So, it's not that we don't have time; it's about taking time and focusing on your priorities.

How do some people take time for God when others don't? They refuse to let anything or anyone push God out of first place in their lives. "But seek ye first the kingdom of God, and his righteousness; and all these things shall be added unto you" (Matt. 6:33, KJV).

## Love God by Giving Him Preeminence

Preeminence is priority's cousin. While priority puts God first, **preeminence** makes Him the most important part of our lives.

If we want to really love God, He has got to be the most important part of our lives. After all, there is no life without Him.

That doesn't mean that you have to spend twenty-four hours a day focused exclusively on Him. But loving God by giving Him preeminence means that you don't allow anything or anyone to be more important to you than God. You protect His time and never let busyness disconnect you from God.

We often deceive ourselves into thinking that we are doing too many important things to have time for God. The truth is that God gives us enough time to accomplish everything and designs our lives with plenty of room for godly fun. We must never believe the lie that we can push God and godly things off until tomorrow. When we fail to give Him preeminence, we're showing Him He's not important enough for today.

No one ever reaches tomorrow, not even the smartest, most talented, and most resourceful people I've ever met. They can't reach tomorrow no matter how hard they try. All we ever have is today, so let's love God by giving Him preeminence. Love Him today. No excuses and no delays.

## Love God by Giving Him Preference

God designed us and knows us better than we could ever know ourselves. God also loves us way more than we could ever love ourselves. That's why His thoughts about the life we live are more important than ours. "'My thoughts are nothing like your thoughts,' says the LORD. 'And my ways are far beyond anything you could imagine'" (Isa. 55:8, NLT).

Our thoughts count but not more than God's. His ways are better than our ways of doing, thinking, loving, and living. It's not always easy to do things God's way, but knowing that His plans for us are definitely the best, we trust Him by choosing His ways over ours. That's called **preference.**

His ways are so much better. If you are going to love God, you've got to prefer His ways, or your love for him doesn't accomplish anything of value. What sense does it make to try to make decisions and find direction on human efforts alone? That's a recipe for disappointment and disaster. The recipe for success prefers His Word over our thoughts, His will over our desires, and His truth over our theories.

That's why Proverbs 3:5–6 can really help us every day. Let's look at it again in a little more depth. "Trust in the LORD with all your heart; do not depend on your own understanding. Seek his will in all you do, and he will show you which path to take" (NLT).

You can love God by giving Him preference every day in every part of your life. He promises that, when you prefer Him and ask for His direction, He will show you which way to go. He may have a teacher recommend you for a special program at school or bring a scripture to your mind when you are trying to make a decision. He loves you enough to lead you even when you don't feel or recognize His presence, and He won't leave you even when you are scared or unsure.

God's power is always bigger than our fear and stronger than our failure, so let's love Him by giving Him preference in everything that we do. So how can you guarantee your A in loving God? Here are some mandatory success points:

1. **Prayer**. Prayer is a spiritual connection with God in which you share, confess, ask, receive, seek, and find more of God. Prayer happens when we **talk with** God and is never us **talking at** God. Prayer is the perfect time to listen to God.

   Yes, God talks to us during prayer, through His Spirit, His Word, and our consciences. Your conscience is the part of your heart that God uses to guide you through what's right and what's wrong like a spiritual compass.

We must have set times of prayer and a continual awareness of God throughout our day to raise our GPAs. Morning prayer starts the day off on the right path. Midday prayer refreshes us and helps us finish strong. Evening prayer allows us to hear God in a special way and prepare for our futures.

God promises in Jeremiah 33:3 to hear you when you pray: "Call to me, and I will answer you. I will tell you great and mysterious things that you do not know." (GWT) God uses prayer to teach us and prepare us to maximize our potential and accomplish our assignments. Turn up your prayer, and you will turn up your success!

Anyone who says he or she loves God but isn't serious about prayer is fooling him or herself, but not God. He knows whether we are serious about loving Him through prayer.

2. **Reading and Studying God's Word.** "All Scripture is inspired by God and is useful to teach us what is true and to make us realize what is wrong in our lives. It corrects us when we are wrong and teaches us to do what is right. God uses it to prepare

and equip His people to do every good work" (2 Tim. 3:16–17, NLT).

It's important to read God's Word every day. It feeds our spirit and guides our thoughts on a godly path. Reading the Bible raises our God-point averages.

It's also critically important to study God's Word, taking time to understand what God was saying to the people it was written for and how we can apply it to our lives today.

God's Word is not a bunch of dead phrases from forever ago: "God's word is living and active. It is sharper than any two-edged sword and cuts as deep as the place where soul and spirit meet, the place where joints and marrow meet. God's word judges a person's thoughts and intentions" (Heb. 4:12, GWT). Reading and studying God's Word builds our faith and increases God's presence in our lives. (Check out John 20:31.)

You can only love God as much as you know God and know about God. No reading and no studying means no love for God. Read and study His Word—you'll have unlimited success. I recommend reading at least one Bible chapter every day.

3. **Worshipping God.** Worship is expressing God's worth while focusing on and bringing positive attention to Him.

You can express God's worth by giving Him praise; telling Him how much you love, appreciate, need, and admire Him; and honoring Him in song and dance or with your other talents.

Worship can happen so many different ways. The important thing is that it happens. And because God is amazing, it should happen a lot! Worship not only raises your GPA, but worship also gets you extra credit. Check out the woman in Matthew 15:22–28. Her worship saved her daughter.

Worship means so much to God. He actually looks for worshippers every day (John 4:23–24). Make sure your worship is maximized with both personal and corporate worship.

Personal worship is when you use your life, individually, to maximize His fame. Corporate worship is when we combine and unify our worship to show God and the world that we love, appreciate, need, adore, and admire Him as our Lord.

4. **Family Connections.** Part of the way we love and honor God is by loving and honoring our natural family.

You may have the greatest family in the world, or you may wonder why God ever connected you to them. Either way, God loves them, and part of the way we show God that we love Him is by helping our families.

It's very important that we respect and care for them. We may not always understand them or want to be with them, but that's when we need to use God's love to forgive them and help them raise their GPAs by following God's plan in Deuteronomy 6. That's where God's Word tells us to talk to our families about loving God with all their hearts, minds, bodies, and souls.

When you honor your natural family, God promises to bless your health and reward you richly even if your family doesn't honor you. So, find something nice to say to them and about them. Look for ways to help at home and pray for your family. Your GPA will rise more than you can imagine!

5. **Church Connections and Service**. Galatians 6:9–10 tells us that there are rewards for God's people who show kindness and bless others. Many of those blessings should flow to your church family

(pastor, leaders, friends, and everyone connected with your church).

If your family isn't connected to a church, it's time to pray and ask God to lead you to the right church quickly. God has a church for you to be connected to and to serve with.

Serving is more than helping or volunteering. Serving others in our church and community is how we show God's love to others and raise our God-point averages. Jesus said in Matthew 23:11, GWT (and Luke 22), "The person who is greatest among you will be your servant."

When we don't serve, we fail, and our God-point averages fall. But when we serve, we soar. When we connect, we climb to wonderful levels of success, maximizing our potential and accomplishing our God-given assignments.

## "God Don't Like Ugly"

Before we leave this chapter, let's raise our God-point averages by eliminating Fs in God. It's not always easy to tell when we are falling away from God, but there are some times when we just know that we aren't right in our actions, thoughts, or intentions. We know we are not loving God or His people.

> Love is not jealous or boastful or proud or rude. It does not demand its own way. It is not irritable, and it keeps no record of being wronged. It does not rejoice about injustice but rejoices whenever the truth wins out. Love never gives up, never loses faith. (1 Cor. 13:4b–7a, NLT)

When we fail to love, we miss God's plan entirely. There is an old saying "God don't like ugly," which means that when our attitudes, actions, intentions, and words toward God and others are hurtful, God is not pleased. "God don't like ugly" isn't proper grammar, but you get the point.

God never rewards pride, boasting, jealousy, or self-centered behavior. God don't like ugly! Raise your God-point average by rejecting ugly thoughts, correcting ugly behavior in and around you, and being a champion for godly love.

—

## Chapter 2 Prayer to Raise Your GPA

Father God, I thank you for showing me your path to success. I pray my love for you and others will have an impact on my reading of your Word, my worship, and my relationships so that I can be close to you. Please help me prioritize loving you, prefer your ways, and give you preeminence in my life in Jesus' name. Amen.

**Chapter 2 Flash Card**

## Your God Point Average

Your God-point average measures whether you are moving closer to God or farther away from Him.

**Chapter 2 Flash Card**

## Loving God with Our All

We love God by giving God
Priority (before all),
Preeminence (more important than all) and ,
Preference (having more value than all).

**Chapter 2 Flash Card**

## God don't like Ugly

Raise your God-point average by rejecting ugly thoughts, correcting ugly behavior in and around you, and being a champion for godly love.

**Chapter 2 Flash Card**

## Success Points

Pray with God, not at God
Reading and studying God's Word
Worship (private and corporate)
Family connection (helping and loving)
Church connection (loving and serving God's people)

## GPA Notes

What does this chapter make you think about?

_____
_____
_____
_____
_____
_____
_____
_____

How can you move closer to God and raise your GPA?

_____
_____
_____
_____
_____
_____
_____
_____
_____

How can you love God with your all?

_____
_____
_____
_____
_____
_____
_____
_____
_____
_____

What ugly thoughts do you need to reject? What ugly behaviors do you need to correct?

_____
_____
_____
_____
_____
_____
_____
_____
_____
_____

# CHAPTER 3

# Your DPA (and What to Do about It)

I n chapter 2, we discussed the **positive** elements that must be in your life to raise your God-point average. So now let's expose the **negative** elements that lower your God-point average and pull you away from God.

"Stay alert! Watch out for your great enemy, the devil. He prowls around like a roaring lion, looking for someone to devour. Stand firm against him, and be strong in your faith" (1 Pet. 5:8–9a, NLT).

I don't like to talk about the devil. No one should like it. But he is our spiritual enemy, and he is looking for ways to destroy people. He doesn't even care who.

Don't make it easy for the devil to pull you away from God. Keep your God-point average high and your devil-point average low!

What is your devil-point average? Your **devil-point average** or DPA measures how much you are helping the devil pull you away from God and setting yourself up for failure. Your DPA measures the negatives in your life.

If you want to get a clearer picture of your devil-point average, look at a few parts of life that separate you from and hurt the heart of God.

## Godlessness: No Evidence of God, No Worship, No Prayer, No Reading, No Fellowship

"Godless fools say in their hearts, 'There is no God.' They are corrupt. They do disgusting things. There is no one who does good things" (Ps. 14:1, GWT).

Imagine if someone told you that he or she didn't believe in gravity. Think about it. You can't see gravity. You can't smell it, taste it, or touch it. You can't even feel gravity. (Falling has a unique feeling, but that is a result of gravity; it isn't gravity itself.)

But if someone told you he or she didn't believe in gravity, you'd know that something was seriously wrong with that person. You'd call him or her foolish, stupid, or worse. It's the same way with believing in God.

There is so much evidence in nature, science, and recorded miracles that God exists. His love shows us that we can live successful lives connected to Him. But far too many people leave God out of their minds, plans, and lives.

Now some people think, "I believe in God, so I'm OK," but there is no evidence of their belief. Godlessness fools us into thinking that it's OK not to pray. It fools us into thinking that it's OK not to read our Bibles, not to connect with other believers, and not to worship God.

Godlessness is a broken lifestyle that rejects God, His authority, and His love. Godlessness is the single biggest boost to your devil-point average, because nothing pulls you away from God as much as pushing Him out of your heart.

The New Living Translation says it another way: "Only fools say in their hearts, 'There is no God.' They are corrupt, and their actions are evil; not one of them does good" (Ps. 14:1, NLT). This shows that when your heart rejects God, evil actions follow.

It reminds me of Proverbs 14:34 as well, in which the Message Bible says, "God-devotion makes a country strong; God-avoidance leaves people weak."

Godliness = High God-point average = Strength
Godlessness = High devil-point average = Weakness

## Cursing/Negative Music Lyrics/Abusing Social Media

"Don't use foul or abusive language. Let everything you say be good and helpful, so that your words will be an encouragement to those who hear them" (Eph. 4:29, NLT); "Avoid all perverse talk; stay away from corrupt speech" (Prov. 4:24, NLT).

You may be looking for some deep spiritual insight on cursing. Let me give it to you straight. Cursing is stupid, and it offends God. Cursing is sinful and an ugly way to express yourself. Cursing pushes your devil-point average up so high that it makes great people uncomfortable to be around you. My mother used to tell me that if you curse, you're just showing people you are not smart enough to express yourself intelligently.

Now I realize some people believe that it's OK to curse when you are super mad or in pain. Here's why that's bogus: it's never OK to offend God, and when you love God, your pain or anger should never push you into sin. Ephesians says, "Be angry without sinning" (Eph. 4:26a, GWT) and Col. 3:8 says "Also get rid of your anger, hot tempers, hatred, cursing, obscene language, and all similar sins" (GWT).

Cursing hurts God every time. Cursing hurts God **every time**. (It's not a typo; I wrote it twice because you need to know this!)

The best way to have a curse-free lifestyle is to follow the direction in Philippians 4:8: "Summing it all up, friends, I'd say you'll do best by filling your minds and meditating on things true, noble, reputable, authentic, compelling, gracious—the best, not the worst; the beautiful, not the ugly; things to praise, not things to curse" (MSG) and hang out with people who don't curse.

When you train your mind to be positive, thankful, grateful, and respectful, your God-point average goes up. But your devil-point average goes up when you think evil thoughts or listen to negative song lyrics that glorify cursing, violence, disrespect, drugs, or sex outside of marriage. Your DPA also goes up when you watch lustful movies and videos and look at ungodly social media content—you know what I'm talking about.

I'm not saying that all of life is positive. There are some hard times and situations that affect everybody. While you can't control what happens to you, you can control your attitude and how you respond to life.

Listening to negative song lyrics, hanging around people who curse, and consuming negative social media help the devil put negative thoughts and words in your mind, making it easier for negative words to come out of your mouth or end up in your texts and social media posts.

Choose to be part of a positive, profanity-free group of friends. Lower your devil-point average by committing to live a curse-free lifestyle and by making your words, texts, movies, videos, music choices, and social media totally positive.

Choosing to be positive doesn't mean you ignore the hard and painful things in life. Being positive means that you focus on being grateful to God and making the most of every situation.

## Dressing Inappropriately

God asks you a question and gives you direction about your body and how you use it in 1 Corinthians 6:19–20, NLT: "Don't you know that your body is a temple that belongs to the Holy Spirit? The Holy Spirit, whom you received from God, lives in you. You don't belong to yourselves. You were bought for a price. So bring glory to God in the way you use your body."

What does that Bible verse tell you? It tells you that your life was designed by God to bring Him glory by demonstrating your love and appreciation for Him in all that you do.

Now we understand that Jesus brought love and salvation (life-giving freedom) for everyone who will believe in Him. That's a major reason why it's important that we dress and present ourselves in a way that allows others to see God's love in our lives instead of flaunting our bodies.

Our DPA rises when we wear inappropriate clothes and dress in a way that brings attention to our sexuality. It's not that you have to be boring and dress like you are a hundred years old. But being young is not an excuse for disrespecting God, yourself, and your family.

Your body and sexuality are gifts from God that should be honored and respected. Your body and sexuality were designed for a healthy lifestyle and a godly marriage, not to be used or abused in ungodly ways. Let's push our God-point averages up by dressing in stylish, appropriate ways. If you still have questions about what is appropriate and what's not, you should ask someone in your church who is well respected and the same gender as you.

## Abusing Drugs/Alcohol/Tobacco: Legal Doesn't Mean Legitimate

There is a list of DPA raisers in Galatians 5:19–21 (NLT): "When you follow the desires of your sinful nature, the results are very clear: sexual immorality, impurity, lustful pleasures, idolatry, sorcery, hostility, quarreling, jealousy, outbursts of anger, selfish ambition, dissension, division, envy, drunkenness, wild parties, and other sins like these. Let me tell you again, as I have before, that anyone living that sort of life will not inherit the Kingdom of God." (Also, check out the GPA building blocks in Galatians 5:22–23 when you can.)

In Galatians 5:20, the Apostle Paul talks about sorcery, a.k.a. witchcraft. The Original Bible language used in Galatians 5 was pronounced *pharmakeia*, which is where we get the word *pharmacy*, a.k.a. the drug store.

Now there are several places where the Bible speaks of plants being used for medicine and healing, so we know that God has created the healing parts of plants and given wisdom for people to create medicines. Sorcery takes the medicines and chemicals that should be used for healing and helping and abuses them to get buzzed, high, baked, smoked, zoned, or whatever word you use to describe the artificially good feeling these chemicals trick your brain into feeling while they destroy your body—the same body that should be a temple for God's spirit, as we learned in 1 Corinthians 6.

Just because certain chemicals and substances like marijuana, alcohol, tobacco, e-cigarette vapor, and some prescription drugs are legal at certain ages in certain states doesn't mean that their use is godly. Abuse of these chemicals and substances pulls you away from God every time—that's why their abuse will always be on the DPA list. Your best life avoids the abuse of these chemicals, and the easiest way to avoid getting addicted and hurt is to never use them in the first place.

Don't let your curiosity or pressure from your peers push you into making life-destroying decisions. Some of these chemicals are so powerful that you can die the first time you abuse them. They are not worth hurting God, hurting yourself, and hurting those who care about you. Stay away from abusing tobacco, marijuana, and prescription or illegal drugs, and if you have abused them, get help to quit immediately. Your future depends on it.

## Premarital Intimacy and Pornography

Let's explore a little more from the DPA list in Galatians 5. The list starts out with the misuse of our God-given sexuality when it talks about "sexual immorality, impurity, and lustful pleasures" (Gal 5:19, GWT). Remember, your devil-point average measures the things that pull you away from God.

When it comes to our sexuality, we are pulled away from God when we use it any time before marriage or in any way that offends God during marriage. There is no permissible or acceptable use of our sexuality before or outside of marriage—**never, ever**. And if you decide to get married, sex is designed to be shared with your spouse and no one else.

We offend God and ourselves when we misuse our sexuality. Sin **always** hurts God and us. Being in love or even engaged doesn't qualify us to use the reward of marriage until we have the covenant (godly promise/agreement) and covering (protection) of marriage.

People often misuse the concept of a committed or exclusive relationship to justify their sexual behavior outside of marriage. The truth is that having a relationship or being in love doesn't equal a covenant, which is designed to last a lifetime. Premarital intimacy is sin, and God will not make an exception no matter how much our desires try to make us believe that it's OK.

Let's be very clear about raising your God-point average by avoiding premarital intimacy or sex. Intimacy or sex is using your body in a sexual way to bring pleasure to yourself or another person. The best way to avoid pre-marital intimacy is to keep your hands off the hot spots. (Hot spots are breasts, chest, behind, thigh, penis, vagina, and whatever else turns you on.) Keep your hands off the hot spots! Keep your everything off the hot spots! That means your eyes, too. Staring at hot spots and the thoughts that follow offend God and push up your DPA. That goes for people in our lives and what we watch on TV, computers, and our phones—everywhere. If you wouldn't watch it with people whom you respect and who love God, you have no business watching it at all.

If you've been struggling with premarital sex, pornog-raphy, or erotic pictures, today is the best day to make things right with God. When I was younger, I struggled with them all. I felt guilty and powerless, and I knew that I was being pulled away from God. Ultimately, it took God's grace, the prayers of my friends, and me making up my mind that I would not offend God or myself anymore to help me commit to being celibate and to stop looking at pornography.

You don't have to lose your battle with your sexual temptations. Here's how to win. The Bible talks about the way to raise your God-point average when dealing with sexual temptations. "Run from anything that stimulates youthful lusts. Instead, pursue righteous living, faithfulness, love, and peace" (2 Tim. 2:22a, NLT).

You weren't designed to win a fight with your own sexual desires. The winning formula is to run away, keep yourself busy with positive godly activities, and avoid the temptation—avoid getting trapped, all while adopting a godly mindset about sexuality.

Keeping it real, the best way to live out 2 Timothy 2:22 and avoid premarital intimacy is to avoid hot situations—being alone with members of the opposite sex. There is no good reason to be alone with someone no matter how godly you think the relationship is. Honoring God is always worth any inconvenience or awkwardness in having others present to help you keep your God-point average as high as possible. It also keeps you safe— too many people have been hurt, abused, or raped by someone close to them or someone they thought loved them.

When someone loves you, they should want God's best for you and not want to use you, abuse you, or hurt you. Abuse hurts, and it's horrible. If someone has abused you or if you were in a hot situation and someone touched you inappropriately or hurt you, please share it with a responsible and caring adult who will help you and support your healing and recovery.

What I am about to share is very sensitive, so I pray that you will understand that it's never OK to blame the victims of sexual or physical assault or to suggest that they are responsible for their attackers' actions. *No al-ways means no. No always means stop.* I share this to pro-tect as many as possible from devastating situations, not to excuse any lack of consent or abusive actions.

On the other hand, there are also some people who have been in hot situations with people they thought wanted to be with them or loved them but later accused them of sexual assault or abuse because they got caught or were embarrassed, ashamed, or scared.

A young man went to college and started to date a young woman shortly after the school year began. The young man thought that they were in love. Unfortunately, they became sexually active. The young woman's parents found out about their sexual relationship and confront-ed her. She was very afraid of disappointing her parents and said that he had raped her so that her parents would continue to support her financially. Her parents insisted on pressing charges, and he was kicked out of his college, went to jail for several months, and must register as a sex offender for the rest of his life. His mother was dev-astated and asked us to pray for him while he was in jail.

YOUR DPA (AND WHAT TO DO ABOUT IT)

Accusations of assault even happened in biblical days. (Read Genesis 39.) A young man named Joseph tried to avoid his boss's wife's improper sexual offers but got caught alone with her in a hot situation, and she accused him of attempted rape. He was thrown in jail and needed God's favor to deliver him. You can learn from Joseph and keep your GPA high by avoiding hot situations.

## Disrespect and Disobedience towards Parents and Leaders

There is another DPA list in 2 Timothy 3:1–5, NLT:

> You should know this, Timothy, that in the last days there will be very difficult times. For people will love only themselves and their money. They will be boastful and proud, scoffing at God, **disobedient to their parents**, and ungrateful. They will consider nothing sacred. They will be unloving and unforgiving; they will slander others and have no self-control. They will be cruel and hate what is good. They will betray their friends, be reckless, be puffed up with pride, and love pleasure rather than God. They will act religious, but

they will reject the power that could make them godly. **Stay away from people like that!**

One of the points that the Apostle Paul wants us to know about our God-point averages and our devil-point averages is that how we treat our parents and leaders determines which averages rise and which averages fall. Parents and leaders aren't perfect, but they are God-given caregivers placed in your life to help you maximize your potential and accomplish your assignments.

God's Word is very clear in Ephesians 6:1–3, NLT: "Children, obey your parents because you belong to the Lord, for this is the right thing to do. 'Honor your father and mother.' This is the first commandment with a promise: If you honor your father and mother, 'things will go well for you, and you will have a long life on the earth.'" The book of Hebrews says, "Obey your spiritual leaders, and do what they say. Their work is to watch over your souls, and they are accountable to God. Give them reason to do this with joy and not with sorrow. That would certainly not be for your benefit" (Heb. 13:7, NLT).

Our goal is to keep our devil-point averages as low as possible. We do that by following God's Word in every area of our lives, including obeying and respecting our parents and leaders.

If respecting and obeying our parents and leaders push our devil-point averages down and our God-point averages up, the opposite is also true. Our devil-point averages soar when we disobey or disrespect our parents and leaders because when we dishonor God's authority in our lives, we are dishonoring God.

I understand that parents and leaders make mistakes, just like you do. It may even seem that they add more hurt than love to your life right now. That's why our job is to be respectful, obedient, and helpful so that our families, churches, and communities can maximize their potential, too. God will reward your respect and obedience.

## Stealing and Lying

Nothing connects you to God more than loving and forgiving. On the other hand, nothing connects you to the devil more than stealing and lying, except maybe murder, which is stealing life.

When it comes to stealing, don't start. If you've stolen in the past, stop it now. God's Word in Ephesians 4:27, NIV says, "Anyone who has been stealing must steal no longer, but must work, doing something useful with their own hands, that they may have something to share with those in need." Your job is to help others and not hurt them by taking from them. Your Heavenly Father will provide everything you need to succeed. Trust Him—He won't let you down.

If you find your devil-point average climbing, the fastest way to bring it down is to tell the truth. Telling the truth puts you back on God's side instantaneously. Jesus said, "I am the way, the truth, and the life. No one can come to the Father except through me" (John 14:6, NIV). He also said that "you will know the truth, and the truth will set you free" (John 8:32, NIV).

If truth leads to freedom, then lies lead to bondage. Lying pushes your devil-point average up because lying rejects the truth from your Heavenly Father and gives the devil greater control in your life.

Jesus revealed the devil's true identity in John 8:44, NLT: "He [the devil] was a murderer from the beginning. He has always hated the truth, because there is no truth in him. When he lies, it is consistent with his character; for he is a liar and the father of lies." If the devil is "the father of lies," then you don't want to mess with his kids. Telling the truth may be hard sometimes, but it's better than offending God and making the devil happy. "So then, get rid of lies. Speak the truth to each other, because we are all members of the same body" (Eph. 4:25, GWT).

## Jealousy/Ungratefulness

I haven't found anywhere in the Bible that says be jealous and always want more. In fact, it says just the opposite in Psalm 100:4, NIV: "Enter his gates with thanksgiving; go into his courts with praise. Give thanks to him and praise his name."

When we are thankful and full of blessing, our God-point average rises. But if we allow jealousy and ungratefulness to take root in our hearts, they grow bitterness and resentment, raising our DPA. God's Word says it this way: "For jealousy and selfishness are not God's kind of wisdom. Such things are earthly, unspiritual, and demonic. For wherever there is jealousy and selfish ambition, there you will find disorder and evil of every kind" (James 3:15–16, NLT).

Having a high devil-point average fueled by jealousy and ungratefulness leads to "disorder and evil of every kind."

That's not the life God designed for you, and it's not the life you want to live. You must reject jealousy and ungratefulness and raise your God-point average through thankful living. "Be thankful in all circumstances, for this is God's will for you who belong to Christ Jesus" (1 Thess. 5:18, NLT).

## Distractions

The devil will do anything he can to stop you from doing God's will. If he can't get you to sin through some of the other areas listed in this section, then he knows that his best weapon against you is distraction. If he can't destroy you, he wants to distract you from your God-guaranteed success.

You may not find the word *distraction* a lot in God's Word, but you will find distraction's origin, temptation, throughout the Bible. Sin and distraction have the same origin—temptation.

All of us deal with temptation. How you handle it determines if you become successful or distracted and whether your God-point average goes up or down.

God's Word makes it plain: "The temptations in your life are no different from what others experience. And God is faithful. He will not allow the temptation to be more than you can stand. When you are tempted, he will show you a way out so that you can endure" (1 Cor. 10:13, NLT). You can keep your DPA low by resisting temptation.

You don't beat temptation by wishing it away, praying it away, or rebuking it. You beat temptation by focusing on maximizing your potential and accomplishing your assignments. Focus on success and follow God's Word in Proverbs 4:25–27 (NLT): "Look straight ahead, and fix your eyes on what lies before you. Mark out a straight path for your feet; stay on the safe path. Don't get side-tracked; keep your feet from following evil." Wow. I love God's Word, and I hope that you grow to love it more every day as you win against temptation and minimize you DPA.

———

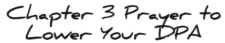

Chapter 3 Prayer to Lower Your DPA

Lord God, thank you for building my faith to resist temp-tation and defeat the devil in my life. I reject godless-ness and everything that tries to pull me away from you. Please help me stay focused on godly success and avoid temptations and distractions in Jesus' name. Amen.

**Chapter 3 Flash Card**

## Godlessness

Nothing **pulls** you away from God as much as **pushing** Him
out of your heart!

**Chapter 3 Flash Card**

## Premarital Intimacy raises your DPA

The best way to avoid premarital intimacy is to avoid
**hot situations.**

**Chapter 3 Flash Card**

## Honor God by Honoring His Authority

Our devil-point average soars when we disobey or disrespect
our parents and leaders because when we dishonor God's
authority in our lives, we are dishonoring God.

**Chapter 3 Flash Card**

## Beating Temptation

You beat temptation by focusing on maximizing your
potential and accomplishing your assignments.

## GPA Notes

What does this chapter make you think about?

_____

_____

_____

_____

_____

_____

_____

_____

_____

_____

What are some of the things that pull you away from God?

_____

_____

_____

_____

_____

_____

_____

_____

_____

_____

What are your three biggest distractions?

_____

_____

_____

_____

_____

_____

_____

_____

_____

_____

In which ways do you need to honor and obey your parents and leaders more?

_____

_____

_____

_____

_____

_____

_____

_____

_____

_____

# CHAPTER 4

## Your Life Matters

Your life matters**—to God, to your family, to your community.

It's important for you to understand and believe that you were designed in Christ to positively connect with and affect others. That's why we feel better when we are connected to the right people, and it hurts when we are disconnected or abused. Your God-point average reflects how well you understand that your life has tremendous value and how personally important you are to God.

The psalm writer, David, wrote it this way: "I will give thanks to you because I have been so amazingly and miraculously made. Your works are miraculous, and my soul is fully aware of this" (Ps. 139:14, GWT). David was encouraged when he thought about the love that God showed him and how He magnificently designed every part of our spirits, our bodies, and our souls. (Also check out 1 Thessalonians 5:23.)

Even though we are designed with love to be winners, every single life has times of pain and loneliness. Sometimes life can be so dark or hard that it seems like no one sees you for who you are or cares enough to notice that you even exist. It can feel like your life doesn't matter to God or anyone else.

Those are the times when you must reach for God's love. Because we can trust God, we can trust His plan to get close to Him. The key Bible recipe is found in James 4:8a (NIV): "Come near to God and he will come near to you."

When you raise your God-point average by loving God and loving others, God blesses you so that your life can bless others. That's when you will truly see that your life matters.

## Your Spirit Matters

Your life comes from God, and your spirit is the God-given force that powers your body and connects you back to God.

One of the most important decisions that you make every day is how you feed your spirit. When you read

God's Word, listen to music with godly lyrics, and connect with God through prayer and worship, your spirit thrives and your God-point average rises.

That's when you will find true happiness, joy, and spiritual power. God did not create you to walk around with your spirit crushed, missing out on true living. God wants you to have a joy-filled life that flows into the lives of your friends and family, while He gets the glory.

Your God-point average goes up when you feed your spirit the right things because you will think the right thoughts, speak the right words, and live the right life. Philippians 4:8–9 shows us that, by thinking godly thoughts and performing godly actions, you will enjoy the presence and protection of the Lord.

## Your Body Matters

Your body is your physical manifestation and allows you to experience the world and interact with other people. While God chose your hair texture, eye color, height, fingerprints, and other physical details, your decisions about your body and your appearance show God and others what you think about yourself and your future.

The scripture that most people discuss when talking about your body and God is one we learned about in chapter 3 from 1 Corinthians 6:19–20 (NLT), which states, "Don't you realize that your body is the temple of the Holy Spirit, who lives in you and was given to you by God? You do not belong to yourself, for God bought you with a high price. So, you must honor God with your body." This scripture shows us that what we do with our bodies, what we put on and in our bodies, where we take our bodies—it **all** matters to God.

Your body is loaned to you by God, and its use is important to Him. That's why the Apostle Paul writes in Romans 6:12–13 (NLT), "Do not let sin control the way you live; do not give in to sinful desires. Do not let any part of your body become an instrument of evil to serve sin. Instead, give yourselves completely to God, for you were dead, but now you have new life. So, use your whole body as an instrument to do what is right for the glory of God."

When you use your body to glorify God, your God-point average soars!

## Your Soul Matters

Your soul is the most important part of you. In fact, your personality, thoughts, mindset, and creative ability are all parts of your soul. Your soul is your inner being that will live forever—it's your spiritual core.

In church and school, you hear a lot about identity—the essence and understanding of who you are. The closer you look at people's souls, the more you see the identity God designed for them. Your soul was important enough for God to create you, special enough for God to love you, and valuable enough for God to sacrifice His Son for you.

Jesus helped us by asking two powerful questions in Mark 8:36–37 (NLT): "And what do you benefit if you gain the whole world but lose your own soul? Is anything worth more than your soul?" Your soul must matter to you—matter enough to prioritize seeking eternal life from God and giving God your best effort in every area of your life. Your soul matters to God, and your God-point average shows God if your soul matters to you, so raise your God-point average.

The reason that you and your life matter to God and those who love you is found in Ephesians 2:10 (NLT), which says, "For we are God's masterpiece. He has created us anew in Christ Jesus, so we can do the good things he planned for us long ago." God uniquely designed you and is preparing you for His purpose. He empowers you to have a 4.0 God-point average with an A in life by caring for your spirit, body, and soul. Remember, an A doesn't mean that you are perfect. It means that you continue reaching toward your best in God and rising with excellence.

God is looking for the **you** He designed—the authentic, amazing you! If you find yourself hurting or suffering from a low God-point average, the time to act is now. Start by asking God to forgive you, and rethink the actions or thoughts that have pulled you away from God. The Bible talks about this when it uses the word *repent*. It means to rethink our lives and our living so that we see life as God sees it.

True repentance leads us to a commitment to live a life that pleases God and turns away from sinful and hurtful living. True repentance also drives us to God through a powerful act of obedience and surrender to Him—being baptized. God's Word says that "baptism is a request to God for a clear conscience. It saves you through Jesus Christ, who came back from death to life" (1 Pet. 3:21b, GWT). If you haven't been baptized yet, please pray about it. Baptism matters to God.

The great news is that God's plan is not just to forgive you. God will empower you through His Spirit to accomplish the great things that we talked about earlier in Ephesians 2:10. Ask God to fill you with His Spirit, and the same power that raised Jesus will raise you and your GPA.

Make your life matter!

Make prayer matter. You'll be connected to God and His powerful love.

Make reading and studying God's Word matter. You'll know more about God and make better decisions.

Make worshipping God matter. You'll find happiness, peace, and joy in His presence.

Make family connections matter. You'll beat loneliness and depression and have help in hard times.

Make church connections and service matter. You'll maximize your God-point average and win with God.

God's purpose in your life is so powerful that, right now, there are people who love you and are praying for you as you turn the pages of this book (or as you swipe if you are reading the e-book). God is strengthening you and building your faith because you matter so much to Him. So, let's get ready for the next times of blessing and testing in your life. When things are great and you feel the love and joy that comes from serving and pleasing God, that's the best time to study for the next life test.

There are also times when life can hurt so much that it feels like we don't matter to anyone or have any purpose at all. It hurts when we feel like we are lonely, lost, and losing at life. I have had more of those times than I can count. We all have.

There are times when we battle depression, low self-esteem, and fear. These hard times can lead to hard questions like "Why do bad things happen?" and "Why does life hurt so much?" When these hard times come, we must rise and remember that we were designed for God's destiny. And when we push past life's pain and focus on God, He'll get all the credit and attention because of your faith and trust in Him.

Let's keep it real—nobody likes pain. But pain can build muscle, pain can build character, and pain makes you stronger when you keep your God-point average high. Our design and our designer show us that the tests and pain cannot override God's power and plan for our lives. God has a spiritual destiny for you. That's why you matter.

You matter because your identity matters. Your destiny matters. Your soul matters. Your body matters. Your spirit matters. Your life matters!

Your life matters to God. Make sure it matters to you!

## GPA Lifeline

There are times when fear, sadness, depression, and loneliness can seem overwhelming. If you have been feeling sad for more than a few days, if bullying seems overwhelming, if you have thoughts about harming yourself or others, or if you know someone who needs help, please connect with your parents, caregivers, spiritual leaders, or school counselors immediately. They are not perfect people, but they really do love you and care about you. They can help you work through hard times better than you can by yourself.

—————

## Chapter 4 Prayer to Maximize Your Life

Father God, thank you for my life. I pray that you would use my times of blessings and testing to honor you and to help me inspire others. Thank you for designing my mind, body, spirit, and soul so that I matter to you and to those who care about me. I ask that you fill me with your Spirit, and please bless my family and church in Jesus' name. Amen.

**Chapter 4 Flash Card**
## Your Life Matters

It's important for you to **understand** and **believe** that you were designed in Christ to positively connect with and positively affect others.

**Chapter 4 Flash Card**
## Your Body Matters to God

What we **do with** our bodies,
what we **put on** and **in** our bodies,
where we **take** our bodies—it **all** matters to God.

**Chapter 4 Flash Card**
## Your Spirit Matters

Your God-point average goes up when you **feed** your spirit the right things, **think** the right thoughts, **speak** the right words, and **live** the right life.

**Chapter 4 Flash Card**
## You and Your Life are God Designed

God is looking for the **you** whom He designed,
the authentic, amazing you.

## GPA Notes

What does this chapter make you think about?

_____
_____
_____
_____
_____
_____
_____
_____
_____

In what areas do you need to be closer to God?

_____
_____
_____
_____
_____
_____
_____
_____
_____

How can you make worshipping God matter more in your life?

_____

_____

_____

_____

_____

_____

_____

_____


How can your life show others that God matters to you?

_____

_____

_____

_____

_____

_____

_____

_____

_____

# CHAPTER 5

---

# How to Win @ School

As we discussed earlier, you are designed for success in every area of your life. One of the main areas of your life right now is school. School helps prepare you for an amazing career and a fulfilling life. School also prepares you to make an impact in this world by using the talents and gifts that God has given you.

After God and your family, school has got to be your top priority. Your God-point average rises when your grade-point average is at its best. Let's talk about some ways to raise your grade-point average and win @ school.

## The Three P3s

The best way to maximize your grade-point average is to start with your attitude about school. School is more than a place to connect with your friends and try to survive the lunches the school serves. School is your opportunity to learn valuable knowledge and develop your professional skills and talents. School is all about preparing for your future, and when you approach school as an opportunity, you'll see that the more you put into school, the more you get out of it.

## Preparation Precedes Possibilities (P3 #1)

P3 is one of my mottos because we never know what blessings and challenges we will encounter in life. But we must be prepared. God is counting on us. God is counting on you.

When I was in college, I was studying engineering for my first degree. I was called into a professor's office in the business school (not even my field of study at the time). He told me he had a one-thousand-dollar scholarship that no one in the business school qualified for, and if I wanted it, it was all mine. No application, no interview.

He searched our school for certain criteria, and my grade-point average qualified me for the money. I left with a check and praise for God. If you read Isaiah 64:4 and 1 Corinthians 2:9, you'll see that God has already prepared amazing things for those who love him. Are you prepared to receive them?

What are you waiting for? Kick your preparation into high gear so that you are ready when your season manifests and your destiny breaks forth. Preparation precedes possibilities. No preparation, no possibilities. Maximum preparation, maximum possibilities. "Jesus said to him, 'As far as possibilities go, everything is possible for the person who believes'" (Mark 9:23, GWT). Will you believe? Will you prepare?

## Preparation Precedes Performance (P3 #2)
Being organized and prepared ensures that when God provides opportunity, you will be able to perform. Remember this—you are not studying to study, practicing to practice, and preparing to prepare. You are studying, practicing, and preparing to perform! God wants your preparation and your performance in the great things He is preparing for your future.

## Preparation Precedes Prosperity (P3 #3)

Proverbs 13:4 (NLT) says, "Lazy people want much but get little, but those who work hard will prosper." If you want it, prepare for it. Winners prepare. Winners prosper.

## A Effort

You control your preparation. You never control the final outcome because God is ultimately in control of everything. So, when it comes to school, your job is to prepare for an A with A-level effort, A-level studying, and A-level focus.

My pastor in college used to say, "Don't study for a C and pray for an A." What I understood him to mean was that it's better to ask God to bless your preparation than to continually beg for His mercy because of your lack of preparation. I'm not saying you can't ask God for mercy—we should, and I do! It's just a much better use of your faith to ask for His blessing as you prepare. Your effort reflects your expectations and faith.

Study for an A every time, and let God handle the outcome. I have never demanded straight As from our sons, but I do demand A effort, and they are glad I do. Both of them are currently 4.0 students. They don't get

As on every assignment and test, but God blesses their A efforts.

A effort means that you check your assignments for errors, and you don't wait until the last minute to do your work. A effort shows your teachers and professors that you respect yourself and them. A effort shows your parents and caregivers that you appreciate all they do for you. A effort prepares you for your best future. Study for an A!

## Study to Learn, Not Only to Perform

When taking tests, studying is key. But it is your approach to studying that makes the difference.

Most of us study to do well on a test or to get an assignment done. If you want to raise your grade-point average, you've got to study to learn. It's a very different approach.

When you study to learn, you begin your learning process before you get to class. Whenever you can, read the lesson **before** the teacher goes over it in class. You are way more likely to understand the lesson, remember it, and do well on tests if you've seen the material before the teachers or professors present it. It guarantees that you will get lost less and understand more. Study to learn—you will raise your grade- and God-point averages.

When you study to learn, you will practice extra problems and research questions from every section you cover. You can't raise your grade-point average by doing only the problems in the homework or on the study guide and believing that you will be prepared for the test. The test will usually be harder and more complex than the homework and study guide—so make sure that you review **all** the material so that you are prepared for any area the teacher may throw at you.

Finally, when you study to learn, you guarantee that you will do better on the final exam. It can be weeks or months between the initial test and the final exam. If you study to learn, you will remember more and find yourself always ready for pop quizzes, and it will be easier to prepare for the final and raise your GPA!

Nobody learns anything by cramming—studying at the last minute, praying for mercy and a miracle. You raise your grade-point average by beginning to study at least three days before every test. That will require you to stay up to date with your classroom websites and apps. Always look ahead to upcoming assignments and tests, and start working and studying as early as you can. You'll do your best work, actually learn the material, and minimize schoolwork stress. That's how our sons have won, and you will win, too, when you get ahead and stay ahead of your deadlines.

## Where Is the Wow?

Average work deserves average grades. That usually means a C. If that is your best, then we'll celebrate your C. But if you are like most of the young people reading this book, your potential is much higher than a C. For you to achieve academic success, you've got to get to wow!

Teachers and professors have to grade so many assignments. Many don't look forward to grading and try to get through it as fast as they can. If your work doesn't give them a reason to grade higher than average, why should they?

Wow goes above and beyond. Wow delivers on the rubric while adding your creative spark. Wow makes your test or paper a joy to read and grade, and wow shows your teachers and professors that you want to maximize your GPA. Don't just get it done. Take the time, and get to wow!

## No Distractions

It's great to want to prepare, want to study to learn, and want to get to wow. But wanting something and achieving it are two very different things. What is the best way for you to maximize your success and achieve your highest God-point average? No distractions.

The enemy of A effort is distraction. For you to produce and achieve, one of the most important things you can do is create the proper environment in your home or wherever you work or study. That environment should have the following:

1. **Proper Lighting**
2. **Supportive Seating.** Or find a comfortable spot on the floor like our sons.
3. **Minimal, Nondistracting Music.** When reading or writing, your best music will be instrumentals.
4. **Sturdy Desk.** Or firm writing area for your best handwriting.
5. **Healthy Snacks.** With plenty of water.

The proper environment should be distraction-free. That means NO

1. **TV and Videos**. Let me make it plain. If you want to have your highest grade- and God-point averages, eliminate TV and videos on school nights. Watching TV on school nights distracts you from doing your best work, studying, connecting with your family, and resting. You often rush through your work, giving C effort or worse, trying to watch something that will probably lower your God-point average anyway.
2. **Social Media**. Is there a bigger distraction than social media? Worrying about someone else's latest outfit, watching the latest cafeteria fight, or seeing your aunt embarrass herself may be entertaining in the right setting—not the cafeteria fights—but all these things distract you from your primary job of raising your GPA. Avoiding social media on school nights gives you the best opportunity to maximize your God-point average and your grade-point average. You know it's the truth. Try it and see what happens.
3. **Video Games**. Are you seeing a pattern here? For the same reasons that watching TV and videos distracts you, video games are double

distractions. They pull you away from your work, and their addictive music and graphics pop into your mind when you are trying to concentrate on your work. Lose the video games on school nights, and enjoy them on the weekend after your work is finished.

4. **Texting.** Save the personal texts and messages until after your work is done. Connecting with your friends is important. It's just not more important than your schoolwork.

## Rest

One of God's greatest creations is rest. Rest is so amazing that even God chose to rest after creating the world. (See Genesis 2.) If rest is good enough for God, isn't it good enough for you?

Seriously, there are some wonderful and rejuvenating things that happen to your mind, body, and spirit when you rest. Sleep is one of the primary ways that we rest. When you skip your sleep, you lower your ability to learn, grow, and enjoy life.

If you are in your teens, your body needs about eight to ten hours of sleep each night. If you are in your early twenties, you need between seven and nine hours of sleep each night. That may sound crazy, but lack of sleep is scientifically proven to affect your mood, behavior, cognitive ability, and academic performance. (See www. nationwidechildrens.org/sleep-in-adolescents.)

You are worth resting for. Take time to rest, and raise your grade-point average!

With God first in your life, do everything you can to prepare, perform, and prosper as He turns the impossible into the possible in your life. Maximizing your grade-point average raises your God-point average and helps you win @ school.

## GPA Lifeline

There are times when you may need help understanding your schoolwork and preparing for quizzes and tests. If you are having trouble raising your grades, please talk to your teachers and family to get the support you need. You may be able to benefit from additional instruction, tutors, alternative assignments, extra credit, studying in groups, and online academic tools. Ask God to guide you and help you maximize your academic potential. Don't give up—rise up with help from God and others.

## Chapter 5 Prayer to Win @ School

Lord God, thank you for the opportunity to learn. I believe that you are using my school and schoolwork to prepare me to prosper. Please help me to study to learn so that I can achieve my best grades. I ask that you help me to avoid distractions and get enough rest to maximize my GPA in Jesus' name. Amen.

**Chapter 5 Flash Card**

## The 3 P3s

Preparation precedes **possibilities**.
Preparation precedes **performance**.
Preparation precedes **prosperity**.

---

**Chapter 5 Flash Card**

## Study to Learn, Not Only to Perform

When you **study** to **learn** and remember more, you'll always find yourself ready for pop quizzes, and it'll be easier to prepare for the final and raise your GPA!

---

**Chapter 5 Flash Card**

## WOW

Wow goes **above and beyond** and delivers on the rubric while adding your creative spark.

---

**Chapter 5 Flash Card**

## You Can Win @ School

Maximizing your **grade**-point average raises your **God**-point average and helps you win @ school.

## GPA Notes

What does this chapter make you think about?

_____

_____

_____

_____

_____

_____

_____

_____

_____

_____

How can you prepare better to win @ school?

_____

_____

_____

_____

_____

_____

_____

_____

_____

_____

What distracts you from giving A effort?

_____

_____

_____

_____

_____

_____

_____

_____

_____

How will you make sure that you get more rest?

_____

_____

_____

_____

_____

_____

_____

_____

_____

_____

_____

# CHAPTER 6

# How to Win @ Life

Success in God is never an accident or a surprise. Success comes from following the godly patterns and directions we find in God's Word so that we can win @ life. Let's look at three of these patterns so that you can maximize your potential and accomplish your assignments.

1. **Win with Bible Recipes**

    Recipes are designed to make great-tasting food no matter who is cooking or how much experience he or she has.

    God wrote down recipes in His Bible so that anyone with a heart for Him can achieve success and win @ life. Recipes like Psalms 37:4–5, Ephesians 6:2–3, Proverbs 3:5–6, Luke 11:9–10, and Isaiah 26:3 all tell of God's great blessings when we follow His instructions or recipes.

One of my favorite biblical recipes is found in Psalm 1. To be truly blessed and have success in everything you do, Psalm 1:1 declares that your first step is to eliminate the influence of ungodly people in your life. You have to have boundaries.

Psalm 1:1 says, "Blessed is the person who **does not** follow the advice of wicked people, take the path of sinners, or join the company of mockers" (GWT). People who do not put God first in their lives and do not worship Him regularly (thereby raising their God-point averages) do not have authority or wisdom to help guide their lives or yours. To keep it real, following the advice and patterns of ungodly people will push you away from God and toward failure every time.

Check yourself before you wreck yourself. Everything that glitters isn't gold. Just because someone says that he or she loves God and calls himself or herself a Christian doesn't mean he or she has a high God-point average. Look for godly success before following someone's advice and before allowing them access to your heart: "Rather, he [she] **delights** in the teachings of the LORD and reflects on His teachings day and night" (Ps. 1:2, GWT).

Psalm 1:2 shows us the secret ingredient in the recipe for a blessed life: loving and thinking about God throughout your entire day. That doesn't mean that every word that comes out of your mouth is about God. It means that God influences every part of your life, and you keep His teachings in your heart and mind, raising your God-point average. That's a major way that you can show God your appreciation for everything He has done.

Now there is a part in each of us that pushes God away and thinks we can be successful by setting our own standards and deciding what God should be happy with in our lives. That's not how the recipe works. The only way that thinking about God throughout your day raises your God-point average is if you are looking for ways to please Him and obey His teachings.

The word that grabs my attention in verse 2 is *delight*, which means to train yourself to find happiness in living according to His teachings. When you delight in God, He rewards you, and

He receives you. You get His presents and His presence. Wow!

"He [she] is like a tree planted beside streams—a tree that produces fruit in season and whose leaves do not wither. He [she] succeeds in everything he [she] does" (Ps. 1:3, GWT).

The third step in this godly recipe shows us God's promise to us when we act in faith. "He [she] succeeds in everything he [she] does." The insight from Psalm 1 is that God honors you when you reach for godly greatness. God blesses our efforts, not our procrastination. He honors our faith, not our fears.

I beg you to fall in love with Psalm 1; your life will **never** be the same. What biblical recipes have you found?

2. **Win with Bible Heroes**

Where are all the real heroes? Are they only in movies and legends?

Like it or not, we need heroes to inspire us, lead us, and rescue us every day. Heroes are not superhumans with special powers. Heroes are regular people who use faith, courage, strength, and righteousness to accomplish amazing things.

Heroes are people we think about and draw strength from when we have a big task ahead of us. Heroes are the ones who sacrifice so others can thrive.

When everyone else backs down and chickens out, heroes step up and save the day. There are many heroes from biblical days—heroes who weren't trying to be heroes. They simply responded to the challenges of their day and did their best while believing that God would help them accomplish their assignments and maximize their potential.

We can learn from all our Bible heroes (Moses, David, Joseph, Joshua, Ruth, Samuel, Jeremiah, Esther, Stephen, Timothy, and so many others), but one hero caught my attention and inspired me while writing this book. His name is Daniel.

You have probably heard of Daniel and how God saved him from being eaten in the lion's den. But have you ever stopped to think about Daniel's success and how he used his talents and faith to please God?

Daniel was like you: talented and gifted in many ways. He lived in a time when God's people had rejected Him, and so that they would learn their lesson, God allowed their enemy to capture them, taking some of their best young people away from their parents and country.

Daniel could have easily let go of his faith and turned away from God. Instead, he courageously used Bible recipes like Psalm 1 and Proverbs 3 to achieve success during hard and sad times. What can we learn from Daniel?

A.  **We learn the value of preparation (remember P3)**

Daniel prepared himself **before** his time of testing. Waiting until the last minute always guarantees that you will do less than your best. The key to preparing is focusing and working on the important things every day.

Chapter 1 of Daniel lets us know that Daniel took care of his body, mind, and spirit. The chosen youth "were healthy, good-looking, knowledgeable in all subjects, well-informed, intelligent, and able to serve in the king's palace" (Dan. 1:4, GWT). Let's break this down a little bit more. The young people who had an opportunity to excel were

i. **Healthy.** They didn't start living healthy lives, eating healthy foods, and taking care of their bodies when their testing began. They must have already been eating well and taking care of their bodies to have been selected for the special training. Taking care of your body is important for you to enjoy your life and be prepared for the opportunities that God will create for you. No one else is responsible for your health but you. Choose the right foods and lifestyle to help you live your best life.

ii. **Good-looking.** We don't know if Daniel and his fellow heroes were handsome or fine, but we know they groomed themselves well and carried themselves with respect. God designed every detail about you, so do your best with whatever body God has given you.

You will look your best when you are showing God's love to the world while taking care of your appearance. Others will see the respect you have for yourself along with your God-given joy and want to know more about you and the God you serve.

While we are all free to express ourselves and our individuality, Daniel and his friends chose to represent themselves and their families with excellence in their appearance. What does your appearance say about how much you respect yourself? God? Your family?

iii. **Knowledgeable in all subjects.** Daniel and his friends applied themselves in all their classes, not just the ones in which the teachers or professors liked them or the classes that came easy to them. You can, too. Colleges, employers, and business partners look for people who are well-rounded and knowledgeable in many areas.

iv. **Well-informed.** They took the time to listen and learn about many different parts of life. They learned the art of negotiation, how to set and maintain priorities, understanding authority, and building business relationships.

Success is never an accident; it is a result of thoughtful preparation. Make sure you learn your schoolwork and learn about the world around you. God wants to use a prepared life.

v. **Intelligent**. Notice that this is different than being knowledgeable in all subjects. There are a lot of people who know a lot of facts but lack wisdom.

There are also people who can do well in school but lack social and emotional intelligence. Intelligence is the capacity for learning, and Daniel and his friends demonstrated that they could and would learn whatever was necessary to be successful. They were committed to learning and doing their best.

You have an amazing capacity to learn and plenty of intelligence. Make sure that you demonstrate your intelligence. Articulate your speech—don't mumble. Make eye contact during conversations— don't look away. Show interest in the subject being discussed through your facial expressions and body language. Don't let your electronic devices distract you in conversations or classrooms. People who demonstrate their intelligence will raise their GPAs and have unlimited success.

B. **We learn the value of obeying and trusting God**

When Daniel and his faith friends trusted God in Daniel 1, they were found to be ten times smarter and better than anyone else.

Their commitment was so strong that they even avoided the king's food and wine to honor their covenant with God. The food may have been ceremonially unclean, unhealthy, or offered to false gods, or maybe Proverbs 23:1–3 influenced them. Whatever their reason for avoiding the king's food, their discipline in their eating and their lifestyle empowered them to be heroes. As a result, God gave them knowledge, wisdom, and the ability to understand all kinds of teaching. When you obey God, you can do better in school and life.

Daniel also received the ability to understand all kinds of visions and dreams. When you trust God and raise your GPA, God unlocks your special talents and abilities to help you serve Him.

Plus, when you obey God, He will cancel out all threats against you. Isaiah 54:17 says, "'No weapon that has been made to be used against you will succeed. You will have an answer for anyone who accuses you. This is the inheritance of the LORD's servants. Their victory comes from me,' declares the LORD" (GWT).

In Daniel 2, the king was ready to kill all the wise men of Babylon. Daniel and his faith friends prayed together and raised their God-point averages to the highest level possible by worshipping God. (See Daniel 2:19–23.) Then God cancelled the evil threat against them.

Do you speak well of God and worship Him? Do you think well of God? We tend to speak about the things we love.

C. **We learn the value of a good reputation**

Check out Daniel's reputation in Daniel 5:12. God gets the greatest glory out of our lives when our high God-point average is seen by and affects others. Remember Ephesians 2:10:

"For we are God's masterpiece. He has created us anew in Christ Jesus, so we can do the good things he planned for us long ago" (NLT).

We touched on Ephesians 2 a little in chapter 4, but this scripture has so much application for your life that you should make it one of your focus scriptures and think about it often. When you "do the good things," people notice that your GPA is rising.

I hope you have heroes—people in your life who care for you, inspire you, and protect you, as well as those who live out their faith with high God-point averages. If you have them, thank God for them. If you don't, ask God to send them into your life and appreciate them when they come.

Have you ever thought that you may be one of those people for someone else? God is looking for heroes. When you have a hero reputation, it allows you to help others raise their God-point averages and achieve godly success. "Choose a good reputation over great riches; being held in high esteem is better than silver or gold" (Prov. 22:1, NLT).

3. **Win with Bible Role Models**

"Remember your leaders who taught you the word of God. Think of all the good that has come from their lives, and follow the example of their faith" (Heb. 13:7, NLT).

You can't be what you can't see. We must surround ourselves with good examples and godly leaders. That way you have a constant, living example from those who live high-GPA lives. Keep them close, and follow their biblical recipes. Before you know it, you'll become a role model for someone else.

In case you were wondering, the difference between heroes and role models is that heroes save you from tough situations, while role models help you prepare for them.

The Apostle Paul wrote to his mentee Titus and told him, "Always set an example by doing good things. When you teach, be an example of moral purity and dignity" (Titus 2:7, GWT). Just like you are watching others, people are watching your life, hoping to see something that will cause them to hope—to believe that God's love can reach them, too. Raising your GPA gives them an example to follow and gives them hope in a better future.

You don't have to be perfect or have perfect answers for their questions; just do your best to raise your God-point average and ask God to help you be a blessing to others.

God already gave you direction to be an example and a role model, so we know that He will give you the strength and wisdom to be successful when you trust Him. "And I am certain that God, who began the good work within you, will continue his work until it is finally finished on the day when Christ Jesus returns" (Phil. 1:6, GWT).

God wants you to win because He loves you and wants to use your life to win others and bring glory to His name. Remember, your success is guaranteed, so use the Bible recipes, Bible heroes, and Bible role models whom He has given to help you win @ life.

———

Chapter 6 Prayer to Win @ Life
Father God, I believe your plans for my life are the best plans. I pray that you would help me use your Bible recipes, Bible heroes, and Bible role models to raise my GPA

and to help me help others. Please stay on my mind and in my heart so that I can make godly decisions and win @ life in Jesus' name. Amen.

---

**Chapter 6 Flash Card**

## Check Yourself

Following the advice and patterns of ungodly people will push you **away** from God and **toward** failure.

---

**Chapter 6 Flash Card**

## Secret Ingredient for a Blessed Life

Loving and thinking about God
throughout your entire day.

---

**Chapter 6 Flash Card**

## Heroes Step Up and Save the Day

Heroes are regular people who use faith, courage, strength,
and righteousness to accomplish amazing things.

---

**Chapter 6 Flash Card**

## You Can Win @ Life

When you stay close to God and raise your GPA,
God unlocks special talents and abilities in you
to help you serve Him and win @ life.

## GPA Notes

What does this chapter make you think about?

_____

_____

_____

_____

_____

_____

_____

_____

Which Bible recipes do you think you should use more in your life?

_____

_____

_____

_____

_____

_____

_____

_____

_____

Who is your favorite Bible hero and why? (If you don't know any, take the time to discover some.)

_____

_____

_____

_____

_____

_____

_____

_____

_____

How can you be a better role model to your friends and family?

_____

_____

_____

_____

_____

_____

_____

_____

_____

# CHAPTER 7

# Extra Credit

Everybody loves extra credit! When you are doing great in a class and you want to impress the teacher, extra credit is the way to go. And when you didn't work as hard as you should have or had a tough time understanding the material, extra credit can help save your GPA.

This chapter covers some fun God-point average–raising secrets that will **maximize your success**. They are small thoughts with big impact that will help you win more and lose less. The thoughts are not intentionally connected or arranged in any special order, but all of them will help you raise your GPA!

## What Do You Want to Be When You Grow Up?

Somebody lied to you. Multiple people lied to you. They may have thought they were helping you, but they lied to you.

They told you that you could be anything that you wanted to be. Now they may have been close to you and probably meant well, but they lied, even if they didn't know they were lying.

The truth is that you will be everything God designed you to be. The lie puts the focus on you and what you think you want, possibly missing out on God's best. The truth puts the focus on God and His plan. The lie says try anything and miss true success. The truth says pray, trust God, and guarantee success.

You will be everything God designed you to be.

"I can do everything through Christ who strengthens me" (Phil. 4:13, GWT).

## Don't Take It Personally.

Don't take other people's hurtful actions and words personally. When other people make bad or selfish decisions, successful people stay focused on overcoming obstacles and achieving their goals, while unsuccessful people focus on "How much they hurt **me**" or "Why did they do this to **me**?"

Now there are some people who may not like you or may not support you in life. So what? There will always be haters and small-minded people. It's different if the hurt comes from family members or dear friends. Pray for them and keep raising your GPA.

You have a choice to accomplish your assignments or perfect your excuses. People make selfish and hurtful choices. Don't be surprised, and try not to get mad. (It's OK to be disappointed.)

We can learn from Joseph in the Old Testament. Joseph wasn't perfect. He believed that God would bless him and dreamed of being successful.

Things were hard for Joseph. His brothers hated him, wanted to kill him, and ended up selling him into slavery. But the Bible says that "The LORD was with Joseph, so he succeeded in everything he did" (Gen. 39:2, NIV). That changes everything.

"If God is for us, who can be against us?" (Rom. 8:31b, GWT). Why focus on who's against you when God is on your side?

Joseph didn't take it personally. He told his brothers, "You intended to harm me, but God intended it for good to accomplish what is now being done, the saving of many lives" (Gen. 50:20, NIV).

Joseph didn't get bitter; he got better. He didn't get depressed; he stayed determined. He maximized his potential while facing tough circumstances, ultimately becoming one of the most powerful men in the country.

You can't control what happens to you, but you can **always** control your response. Nobody makes you sin, makes you mad, makes you curse, or makes you do anything. You choose your response, and you alone are responsible for your actions. "Do not let sin control the way you live; do not give in to sinful desires" (Rom. 6:12, NLT).

## It's Not "What's Wrong with It?" It's "What's Right with It?"

A while ago, I was having a talk with one of our sons. He wanted my permission to go somewhere or do something (I don't even remember what it was), and when he realized that I was about to say no, he said to me, "But Dad, what's **wrong** with it?"

Without thinking, I asked him, "What's **right** with it?" My answer (it was really a question) made him think. When we ask "What's wrong with it?" we focus only on our present and not our potential.

God has so much prepared for us that we cannot afford to make decisions based only on our current circumstances, pleasure, or pain. "What's right with it?" forces us to see whether the choices we are making help us raise our GPAs or lower them. Do they get us closer to God or pull us away from Him? This applies to relationships, college choices, eating choices, tattoos, piercings, sports, credit cards, roommates—**everything**.

Too often we look for the absence of negatives rather than the presence of positives. Think about that.

Like in relationships. I often hear young people trying to justify relationship choices by saying "He doesn't smoke" or "She doesn't curse," as if the fact that someone tells you that he or she doesn't have foolish habits makes it OK to be in a relationship with that person.

We must look for the presence of positives—the "What's right with it?"—in relationships. Does your potential partner actively love God and not just say so? Does he or she worship Him regularly? Is he or she kind, respectful, faithful, patient, helpful, responsible, celibate, and thoughtful?

For everyday living, here are some things to think about when deciding "What's right with it?"

- Is it sinful or negative? If it is, it's not right for you and has no place in your life.
- Does it help others, or is it a purely selfish desire?
- Does it fit the Philippians 4:8 model? If not, it shouldn't be on your mind, much less in your life. (See chapter 3 for the Philippians 4:8 model.)
- Do godly people who care about you think it's a good idea?

A few months later, I was trying to get the same son to try something, and I asked him, "What's wrong with it?" He smiled coyly and asked me, "What's right with it?" I think I've taught him too well!

## Dreams Don't Come True.

Dreams don't come true—plans come through.

What's the difference between a dream and a plan? I'm glad you asked. A plan is written down with thoughtful details and timing. A dream is talked about and fantasized about but never becomes real until it's written down and planned. Everything changes when you think it through and make a plan.

Remember, dreams don't come true—plans come through. **Write it down!**

## Relationship Deal Breakers

If they won't be celibate while single, why should you believe they'll be faithful when they get married?

If they won't be faithful in their current relationship, why would you believe they'll be faithful in their next relationship?

I've heard it said that if they cheat with you, they'll cheat on you. If they'll do it with you, they'll do it to you.

On the flip side, if **you** are not trying to please God while you're single, what makes you think that you will try to please Him when you get married? I'm just saying...

## Friendship and Relationship Reality Check

How can you tell if people are really your friends and genuinely interested in you? Don't be impressed by attention. Be impressed by investment! There is a difference between someone who is being friendly with you and someone who is willing to be your friend. Classmates, neighbors, and coworkers can all be friendly, but people aren't true friends until they truly sacrifice something for you (time, money, effort, etc.). You are gifted and loved by God and will have the right number of genuine friends if you don't let fake friends use up your life. People show you what's important to them by how they invest their time, money, and effort.

It is also important to build friendships and relationships with godly people. They aren't perfect, but as Psalm 1 shows us, ungodly people don't succeed: "For the LORD watches over the path of the godly, but the path of the wicked leads to destruction" (Ps. 1:6, NLT). That doesn't mean we should be mean or disrespectful to anyone who isn't living a godly lifestyle; it just means he or she isn't prepared to be a true friend or have a deeper relationship with you.

## GPA Relationship Note

Respect is free, but trust is earned. Respect honors a person as a fellow human being and as someone God loves. Trust is totally different. Trust is built, nurtured, and protected by being **consistently** truthful, honest, and faithful. Trust is absolutely necessary for relationship success and must be earned over time—never given. Anyone who wants to be your friend or says "trust me" without earning your trust is not qualified to be in a relationship with you or to have access to your heart.

## Don't Try to Be Smarter Than the Bible.

God's Word is special and reveals the heart of God (how He feels) and the mind of God (what He thinks). God knows everything about everything. And when He gives promises, direction, guidance, and warnings, our choice is either to obey or disobey Him, to trust Him or reject Him.

Don't try to outthink God, rethink for God, or outsmart God. You're not smarter than God, so don't try to be smarter than the Bible, His Word, and His plan.

As you understand more of God's Word, do your best to live it. Don't waste your time trying to justify disobedient behavior or why you think God's way is wrong or outdated. God's way is the **best** way—and the **only** way to raise your GPA.

———

## My Prayer for You

I may not get to meet you personally, but I would love to hear from you (@raiseyourgpa). I am confident that the thoughts in this book will help you find true success and joy in God. Here's my prayer for you:

Heavenly Father, I thank you for the privilege of sharing the thoughts you gave me with the incredible people reading them right now. They may know exactly who you've designed them to be or, like I was at their age, have no clue at all about the future, but they have hope that you will help them succeed.

I know your love for them is greater than any power they have ever experienced and that your love will bless their spirit, soul, and body. Help them to trust you now, love you now, and live for you now and forever.

Thank you for guaranteeing their success and forgiving their mistakes. I ask that you guide them as they raise their GPA so high that their success affects the people in their lives and that you get all the credit in Jesus' name. Amen.

Your journey to winning at school and life begins now! Write your own GPA prayer to God on the next page to empower you and inspire you as you rise. God bless you.

Jonathan

---

# My Raise My GPA Prayer to God

## GPA Notes

What does this chapter make you think about?

_____

_____

_____

_____

_____

_____

_____

_____

_____

What dreams do you need to create a plan for and write down?

_____

_____

_____

_____

_____

_____

_____

_____

_____

_____